Out of Lethe

poems by

Dan Cullimore

collected and edited by **Victoria Holtz Wodzak**

Finishing Line Press
Georgetown, Kentucky

Out of Lethe

Copyright © 2020 by Dan Cullimore
ISBN 978-1-64662-145-3 First Edition
All rights reserved under International and Pan-American Copyright Conventions. No part of this book may be reproduced in any manner whatsoever without written permission from the publisher, except in the case of brief quotations embodied in critical articles and reviews.

Publisher: Leah Maines

Editor: Christen Kincaid

Cover Art: Luke Wodzak (lwodza20032@outlook.com)

Author Photo: Lee Cullimore

Printed in the USA on acid-free paper.
Order online: www.finishinglinepress.com
also available on amazon.com

Author inquiries and mail orders:
Finishing Line Press
P. O. Box 1626
Georgetown, Kentucky 40324
U. S. A.

Table of Contents

Ars Poetica 1
This Daimon 4
Astronomy Lesson 6
In a Night Café 7
The Cat Knows How 8
Narcissus Discovered 9
Before Wandering 10
Song for His Children, Left Behind 11
Glossolalia 13
With Some Small Guilt 15
The Code 16
To Be Faithful 17
I'll Take My Violets White 18
Irrefutable 19
Reading Magazines in the Car Coming Home 20
Oranges 21
To Lust, Without Apology 22
Monday, January 18, 1999 24
A Song 25
Heaven 26
The Birth of Tragedy 27
Perhaps 28
Remembering Hiroshima 29
Spring Evening 30
Winter Windows 31
Labor Awaits the Muse 33
The View From Spring 34
Hidden in Books 35
What Might Have Been 36
What We Call Seeing 37
A Pocketful of Sand 38
Epiphany 40
Remembrance 41
Honoring the Ancestors 42
Eureka: Archimedes Remembers His Mother 44
He Leaves This 45
Last Wish 46

Ars Poetica
    (Triptych)

I.

A poet wants words
fragrant as a fading hour
under nearly subtle cedar—
the sun cooling,
the moss and mud
(that prickled smell
where green rusts)—
the deer-shaggered shelter
fluttering, breathing
deep in the turning season;

words to carry home
a husk of light,
shadowy on goose-winged paths;
words
fletched and undulating
as long-stretched arrows
of beak-nosed necks;
words that stutter
a polar-pendant sermon
into silence,
echoed and honked out
in city-pitying piety;

persimmon-seeded words
rough barked as their bearer,
bitter as inexperience,
ripened orange in sweet frost;
words that glisten—
red-jeweled,
studded,
simple—
forsaken beside a path
like possum shit, or

sub-cutaneous as blackberries
bear-beaten since summer,
honeyed
and ripening now into fuel
beneath thick black fur,
thick with grubs, roots,
anything
that burns tomorrow
in slow mimic of the sun;
words that sleep all winter and wake up hungry.

A poet wants words
useful as nuts.

II.

I work to tongue some piece of being
into being. Sometimes certain
of a truth, mostly just uncertain. The urge
to mouth is more,
enough—
to mouth and word
the blank before me
into shapes,
to move a shape of lines,
to urge on shifting shapes
a cursive grace and draw
from lines so old
and commonplace their art
has been forgotten. (What art
is more abstract or absolute
than this
ephemeral cuneiform? A mark
to make the stoic image real;

a standing wave that handed down
the line will stand instead
for shapeless things
which live and slip
in synapse' space,
that distance
between nerve and time; a hope
that dry and airless forms
fly, moving moist and quick,
the distance between fact
and faith.) So much depends
upon no other speech.

III.

The weight of this line follows the distant curve
of this world. We don't see it bend;
it lies plumb on the page, level
as the space between two points (gravity's
the softest, most insistent fact
in the visible, the invisible
bone that bends backward upon itself
every being, even this flight voice
insistent in its air).
Bent to any other shape it falls
as tongues so often fail in age
to meet the mind;
some fault fissures
open upon nothing
sensible, the language shaken,
a path rendered
useless as a word apart,
a poem.

THIS DAIMON

Out of Lethe we fall, wet with forgetting
down from cloud light into teeming time,
precious with labor, rooted
in cherried darkness,
In gasping
we grasp it, shitting
and grubby
all the way.
                  Home,

where they close the door and turn the furrows.
They plant and cut, knead and burn,
drink and rut and dance and
name the fruit of fucking
after us, if we're lucky.
                  It's a life.

In time, amnesic need unfurls into childly
we learn to sink
dust into dust, seedwise, and simple.
There's water enough and light,
breezes yellow with buzzing
and pollen—pregnant.
We're stubborn to stay, find
in reliance
a lesson of necessary neighbors,
commit to study how prairies live,
lightening-struck,
in burnt-over roots,
                  all ramshackle.

The purposed pattern always down,
fretfully, fatefully
by necessity down. The body knows
how carbon cycles, death wrinkles to feed it, nitrogen

up-takes only to collapse. Birthing's our cast-aside
call to wisdom: grief
                    make it useful.

The wit to wizening left in nowhere waters,
except this daimon who sits beside us, alive
as any hand we'd grasp.
Unasked

Although the debt's repaid
(for former leading leant)
by late acknowledgement,
and muscled labor, laid
upon the scale it bent
toward the soul's handmaid,
and weighed my true desire:
I'd a mentor of him wanted.

Like Merc'ry, fleet as fire,
the Gods, unknown but hunted,
unimaged, only wanted,
fly swift before they sire,
leaving knowledge stunted.
Wait makes of want a liar;
my questions, newly made,
unasked, remain unspent.

By other coin is hope repaid,
and succor to this heart is sent.
Sleep by that voice clear is rent,
and intuition comes to aid.
No longer are these cars for hire,
but inward peer for all that's said.
By this voice I am enchanted.
By soul, my mentor, I am afire.

Astronomy Lesson

A ring of light burns
just beyond eyesight.
Practice tracing it. Chalk
halos like an artist,
in the air above every head.
Stop looking into mirrors
(don't wait to be convinced;
there is no proof
sufficient).

We know stars glittered
in galaxies so removed
that time and distance
lose conviction.
Their bent and blush refuse
to condense on glass.
What was must be imputed,
our knowledge
of that noumenous light
conjured
from inaudible impulse.
What is must be converted,
miracle, as at a wedding—
silent sound changed
into light, water
into wine.

There is a ring of light.
Draw it with your will,
an invisible holy circle
neighboring every face.

In a Night Café

Sitting here, I can see
street lights flash
off the polished paint
of fenders and trunks
like mechanical stars.

There's a woman's voice
in each ear,
girls giggling
with divine secrets
in their eyes,
and I am drunk with longing.

If you take offense when I stare,
I'll ask you to turn off
your beauty.
You're distracting me.

The Cat Knows How

This cat is as insistent as new love
and surely as full of folly.
Not content sitting in a lap
of absent-minded strokes,
he climbs the chest on persistent paws,
nuzzles the chin,
purrs through veils of hair
as if whispering
secret desires through a curtain.

All the while, my wife of seven years
and I
argue
about not getting what we want.

Narcissus Discovered

What did old Tiresias say?
That he'd live to old age
if only he never knew
the moist complexion of his own face?

What death, then, was it he found,
staring at that beautiful boy?
How many Echoes did he refuse along the way
thinking, *gods must speak in foreign tongues?*

At what age did he finally leave the path,
sit on the cool untrod earth—
and paradise dark in waters
beneath the trees?

Was it hunger kept him quiet
and breathing like a monk,
legs folded like Buddha,
leaves mounting as snow upon his shoulders?

How hard the breast-blow
striking the fire?
Mighty thunder from Zeus,
or the kindling crack splitting in the wood?

Or softer still,
flint on steel,
or the spark that flies
when seeing true friends?

What would you refuse, what blow swallow,
to see the *I Am* inside "I am"?

Before Wandering

I could have used that knowledge
years ago,
before the years of blood and wandering
before I became an arsonist of the heart,
firing hoes around me, sending
acrid incense up
toward the gods,
before finding myself kneeling
in ashes
before the altars of regret.

I want to know what kept Penelope
skeining her yarns while he toiled
before the Fates. What sign
before the door post
made the angel pass over?
What kept their home
through the heat and the cold absence
of attention?

because here I am again
feeling that pull after Helen,
the need for action hot and final,
a torch in my hand,
a baby crying at my back.

Song for His Children, Left Behind

I.

So well you know me,
all I've been:
>that I leave too early,
>that if ever I arrive
it will be too late;

>that this fractioned absence
>is less than bearable,
>that it requires an oil
>we've never had;

that to ease the bearing,
smooth the binding, means
all I've ever been
>must change.

II.

I think it not enough to say
I was afraid.
The vacancy gifted you
you have filled,
and what is there is more
than I would have known
how or why or when
to add.

To say this only confirms the truth—
I was afraid,
and as I've said,
that's
not
enough.

III.

Any poverty I could claim is
nothing
to the nothing you have known.
No wealth in this verdant world
could spring those invisible voids,
so this is no coin to jangle silently
in that poor pocket you inherited
        (and perhaps still wear in not
        false
        but fearful hope).

If in keeping *this*
some small bell you hear,
dig a little deeper,
risk the price of hope,
knowing
even empty winter ends.

IV.

Even these words serve me,
my purpose,
my grief,
at your expense?

Tell me so,
and this mollusk tongue
will eunuch itself
              to silence.

Glossolalia

Six or seven men around a fire:
gravity-shadowed, they sit, circling
the heart heat at the core.
Stars leaf through wheeling trees.
Deer, or fox, rim beyond the reach
of dancing light. An owl tells all.
A myth: here, only magic happens.

In this crucible
of words and light,
each man talking, turns: a spoke
through which arcs
leaping and ashen language
older than any chalice, any blade,
any other tongue.

They come knowing stories,
carry something
               broken,
live openly in their secrets,
tremble under memories, like Moses knowing
    from a burning bush
        Jehovah breaks the silence.

They come
to turn the stone of some old law,
lift the grists of grief and joy,
and grind, on ancient tablet
unbroken by the Momus calf,
their chaff-full lives;
from this they bake, and break the bread.

They eat their fill. They do not rush,
but see in circling discipline and fire some hope:
potters who calcine squalid clay,
knead and shape the lump,
dip muddy hands into the slake
and smoothly slip the pot upon the wheel,

…these make a better void.
It is this vessel for which they've come.

Men sit around a fire and talk.
They eat and end up empty.

With Some Small Guilt

With some small guilt one wonders
how they companion themselves—
the abandoned, the grief eaters,
the survivors of suicides.
One thinks (a pride!) that
in their aloneness
whatever sustains them is,
must be,
that which drove
the pulse-parting blade;
or drew the bight taut 'round trachea,
suppling bone and sinew with a snap;
or with narcotic strength closed hard
the blighted windows,
blotting out the troubling skies.

So little compassion,
until one recognizes that
in each generation
any body
can carry the madness
and it is no large feat that
before fate we are each
hapless,
and equally.

The Code
(Upon witnessing a woman die, her hand in mine)

Just a week before, a friend said
that he'd heard
the rattle of death,
like a code,
at the moment of collapse
(like bones, I wondered,
like a cipher?)
"You never forget it," he said.
I tried to imagine.

At forty, I'd arrived
with only vague, privileged
intimacies—
grandparents passing long
before my unripe remembering
began,
some dim face in a yearbook,
the father of a friend long outdistanced
(though synapse holds tight this eloquence,
his nonsense of a hand
flailing overhead for days before he went),
—kept from that ancient intrigue
by secreting innocence.

Tonight, boyhood abandoned me.
I heard that rhythm
rattling like soft mashing cymbals
in the body's mouth,
the soul banging on tooth's door;
a dog rampaging in the hall.
It keeps me awake,
baying and scratching in my mind.

Now I have memories;
the code is broken,
and I am a spy.
Where do I hide?

To Be Faithful

These are hard words:
"Let the dead bury the dead."

There is no middle road,
look for it as you will.

If you really want to know
the steps in Lazarus' dance,
you should remember the fate
of lukewarm swill.

Of course, being spat from the mouth of God
is better
than never to have been drunk in the first place,
but why not stay
and make the Old Man weave?

I'll Take My Violets White

The violets round this house are blue
no more.
Still there in full and future bloom,
and just as green of leaf,
but something in their skin has been

forgetful. Or
maybe is is really mime,
and they mimic with this white
the winter snow
and cold on skin.

That unseen fist of color
recollects in sanguine sheen
and hides—sun-shy and cyanic:
the blue remains as blood
in veins.

I remember reading why, but can't recall the reason:
if it's failure in the sky above,
or something wrong in last year's season
(maybe more manure would restore
their virgin blue).

I'd find that book in which I'd find
this mystery resolved, but why
I'd want to pull this root anomaly
escapes me. I'll take my violets white
and miss their paler-pansy hue.

The irises are coming on,
the spiderwort is up. It is
still spring, and all of summer yet;
there's time enough
for blue.

Irrefutable
    (for Sally)

It's just our usual evening stroll,
but from the castle of my shoulders
she speaks the irrefutable,
and while our shadows
stretch tall
or fall behind under white street lights,
her four year voice
descends to my soles
and deeper,
"Daddy, I'm bigger than you!"
and I'm convinced
this is the only truth
worth knowing.

Reading Magazines in the Car Coming Home
(for Ibtisam)

Early afternoon
sun slants lazy across the page.
As one friend drives
and sings with the radio
another, his wife,
sits and sleeps.
The words dance
crisp, black,
alive.

The back seat a tangle
of legs, knees, laps—
your body mingled with mine.
Last night's aroma,
still working its way in,
becomes part of today,
transfigured by memory
and sunshine.

You hold my hand to your face,
and I see
grass greening under old snows
lining the highway outside.
This light
shows everything.

Oranges
       (for Ashbery)

Language can be
brilliant
new oranges, even
as a woman soiled
in denim
carries (wooden,
worn as words,
a ladder)
the conversation
lagging.

Bright fruit plucked down,
Pin cushion
skin and warm, this
tolerable rape with the neighbors
shouting
their common history, all
within an ideal fraction of light:
green looks different, too,
to the faceted bee.

Of necessity we skip the missing rung.
This will not matter.
Bitterness is,
or the orchard opposite of oceans.
It still absorbs all other waves.
Meaning is held so briefly,
then eaten.
All fruits are
broken things.

To Lust, Without Apology

With other men I share a race
and see with now unhurried haste
what lives upon
and shines within our face.

It is a trace we cannot hide,
a sting,
a lace,
a prick denied,
our commonplace,
our mammon will,
                our pride.

Truth be told, we've lied
about this wound,
and hoped, or tried,
convinced a boon
awaited us in pied
flesh, that faithless swoon
where bitter sound
the feckless bells—
        On thin ground,
           thin ice before the fells!
—a din compound
forswears with empty knells
what in these bloody tells
remains of ancient men:
our very cells
confirm and ken
what jells and jekylls,
        what some call sin.

It's only when our bones break old,
our blood thin and growing cold
that hides within a brain still bold
thoughts of green, and tales untold
of   spring eternal,
            our strength diurnal;
            our lives unsold,
            the sun still gold,
the world?
            —still vernal.
Let's praise this chase.
Men come round and sing in brace
our common hound, this grace
we feel too soon unbound,
that we could know our freedom found,
in truth, and in honor do our common
            ground.

Monday, January 18, 1999
   (rfk)

Blotches of brown will become green
Emerge through the melted snow.
Rivulets of water flow down the hills.
The woman who drives the car,
Carefully gages the speed and feel of the wheel,
As she goes between remaining snow banks,
Around the bend in the road on the hill.

The wind is strong, is cold.
Is better to leave errands for another day.
No mail today, a holiday it is
Because of a man named King, who stormed
        for the rights of his people up to the end.

In retrospect,
        when is there a holiday for others oppressed?
The Jewish People, the immigrant Irish,
The Spanish descendants who were here first,
The Indian Nations so utterly betrayed.

The isolated woman on the hill,
Sits to watch the 6:00 news.
She shuts her eyes for a bit
Opens them to find there was no news.
She has a friend, Helen,
        who oft has the same experience.
Can you explain it, this bit of hypocrisy
        on the part of the Media?

Did she do her self-appointed tasks today?
Not really—One day leads to another
With nothing of importance to relate.

She daydreams as she thinks of time to be spent
With grandchildren and a special friend.
Of the tour that is planned when summer begins.
                    finis

A Song

The strings on this heart
are too often silent—
a guitar hung for show
on the wall.

there are nimble fingers
that know completely
the paths symphonies take
when falling from the billion suns,
and can count the rhythms rising,
perfect as spheres,
from the iridescent depths.

Sometimes I think the mistake is mine.
I could have been a better student,
spent more time playing scales,
counting beats,
discipline as elusive to me
as Beethoven's ears.

And then I think
perhaps it is enough
to keep it tuned,
and pluck out simple melodies
in celebration:
the able hands of a good friend,
wrinkled cheeks curved expectant
toward a kiss,
the solid light in my boy's eyes
when he knows it's enough
just to hear
the song of his own name.

Heaven

Heaven fell flashing on the mist,
and searched, 'tween paling fruits, a mate,
confirmed, with signal lights, the tryst,
whilst I upon this dance with Fate
fell bound, and still the spell persists.

'Tis easy to believe in Fairies' state,
lose Reason when Reason argues late.
Against such beauty it can't resist,
and Will or Faith both powerlessly insist
on something more than meets the eye.

It's enough to stand with mind a-gate
and witness earth entwined with sky.
What knowledge knots, these sights untie.

The Birth of Tragedy

The spiders' bite is just as deadly
at the edges of the web. It's only we
who flinch and enter preconceived.
A fly at center's given up
for lost, but the edgewise fly we favor,
holding out for staged machines,
what in this dispensation could only be
ungodly.

But deadly is not right. Initially
narcotic, only later does the caustic work.
Then flies dissolve into whatever dream it is
that fly-mind can conceive, are wrapped
and set aside—a sack of life
for later living. That bite is really mercy
at its best. It's we who make up other tales.

This scene enacts itself into the future,
with memory slipping like a thread
the eye of truth. What that web never was
becomes—whole cloth—a possibility,
and though the noose is seldom
slipped, we wrap the future up in hope.
It's weavers' knots that clothe our lives,
our knowing what we know.

Perhaps

All of the windows in the house
At the top of her hill
Have been smashed. Now
Drapes flap outside
Their sashes and the memories
That lived there
Trade places with birds.
She tells everyone stories

The birds leave behind—no one
Believes. Perhaps
They fear her, now
That she no longer
Trusts the man who—
For sixty storm-proof years—
Also wintered in those rooms;
Perhaps it's pity,

Because they know
She didn't willfully
Smash the glass, hasn't
The skill to fix stained
Carpets, the rotting plaster;
Or, perhaps, just because bird song
Sounds truest
When sung
By birds.

Remembering Hiroshima
(memento mori, mement ut vivas)

The grass is dark
and dewy against our toes.
We four walk, holding hands,
around the long, black lip
of the unrumpled lake.
Waveless in the summer-heavy air,
it holds a suburban incandescence,
orange and sulfur-white,
sailing, reflected, at mid-distance,
and the softer,
more distance-dimmed lamps
of heaven,
limpid and radiant overhead,
and the lanterns,
handmade and candled,
afloat now against forgetting,
frail reminders of artificial stars,
handmade and fissile,
burst to burn,
and bury,
cities,
and of sleepers who no longer dream
under the ancient edge
of sun-rising skies.

A frog leaps,
ghost-white
against the dark and dewy grass,
leaps
for its life
toward the lit and burning lake.

Spring Evening

Fireflies were out last night,
sparking the shadowy grass
beneath absented stars.

An approaching storm secreted
everything
but the flies' chaotic twinkling,
and the sunlight dying
in the dusk high above,
and the smell of spring flowers in the wood,
and the creek sound.

Even the moon's full bosom dressed,
glowing behind dark lace
raggedly tatted by the skittering clouds.
No modesty there, however.
She was wanton in her privacy,
knowing, no doubt,
that in his passion
the thunder would hide her from all but his eyes.
Small wonder.

Winter Windows

The winter windows are beautiful
in this early morning café,
glowing with beaded light,
stippled, steady, streaked
by slow falling stars,
telling tales by degree of difference
of gravity,
of mass and energy,
the beautiful physics
of cold reality.
It's the story of anger in the human heart.

Sit in this chair,
a table by the window,
the glass holding imperfectly in
the marvelous light,
sweet tea and cakes,
slight chills made comfortable
by warm laughter,
all kindly familiar,
all tenuous behind this security
so easily shattered,
so uncertainly fixed in the firmament.

But this morning there is no errant
baseball,
no well-aimed brick,
merely degrees of difference,
the tilt of the earth,
slant of energy falling
so softly from a star
as to be normal,
expected,
even appreciated,
and the glass,

glazed by unnumbered evidence,
securing only the wanted
from the unwanted.

Can science parse this division?
Is it subject to formulas,
experiments,
the judgment of experts?
What has physics to say
about hot and cold,
the placement of stars,
slant of seasons,
when there is this filter
between the wanted
and the unwanted,
when a single word
is a brick,
and a glance
changes the path of planets?

Still,
the light is beautiful
behind these winter windows.

Labor Awaits the Muse
(or: Procrastination)

Rain all night,
sleeping weather rain,
and this morning,
he's reluctant to go to work,
though the clouds cleared early
and a lemon sun
tosses out cool invitations—
no rolling sweat
will blind the aiming of spades today.

He fears the weight of clay;
knows that, unlike thirst,
it's no lighter for the slaking.
Earth is like any other flesh:
the deeper one digs,
the harder's the digging,
until the point reaches bone,
and steel dulls,
refuses to cooperate;
rain only adds weight
to density and depth.

He wonders why God
or nature
made this hard life thirst,
as if it weren't enough to carry,
around these dry bones,
dense clay. ("Hard
enough to budge,
without that mass and mess.")

And so, he
holds out for drier times,
resists the digs of guilt,
pushes something weightless and almost wet
across a dry, unsoiled page,
hoping clouds will burst.

The View from Spring

Walls. Of voices built. Mossed
inflection of bricks, barbs of tongues
wounding, innocent as the rose
climbs, ignorant, perennial (sounds
and sloth) pricking the ear,
angled for a tender thing
open and biding
behind its untried audition.

Some garden that childhood
watered—rose red and bleeding
hearts dead on the vine, fertile
as virgin dirt to the harlot seed.

It's a deed done. One garden,
brick walled, and nothing
grows in winter.

Hidden in Books

The famous and dead
have written books
about what you know bone deep.
Mumming blankness into bodies
they buried black bones
within a paper tomb.

The man you seek,
the one who wants your prayers,
is libraried, catacombed
on shelf of would-be kings,
his heart, pharoah's perfect token,
embalmed in a jar of clay.

What Might Have Been

There's a path none living ever walks,
though what heart hasn't
skipped on strong strides
that swift, smooth stretch
to the inevitable curtain,
and seeing beyond
with chimera-certain eyes,
sighed, or wept,
or like Moses sweating in the dust,
given thanks
for what was promised.

What We Call Seeing

If we hold our gaze on one thing alone
       what else happens?
At what age do we grind our lenses fine
and polish the prisms of attentions,
learning the proper attitudes
for casting scattered rainbows
across the walls of memory?
When do we discover the idol-mastery of
flash and spangle,
leaving outside the white light
under which we lived so transparently?

Do we keep these sightings without question,
or can we plug coins
of hope and desire
into different slots,
as on those telescopes atop tall buildings
though which tourists divine the city below,
a city which locals,
without need of maps
or larger visions,
ply like ants?

A Pocketful of Sand

His mother's a smooth-rimmed lake.
Even calm, she's inscrutable.
Anything reflected there is changed—
trees hung from their roots,
mountains suspended as in dreams.
Intuition in her depths falters
like the fading descent of the sun
'til at bottom
it's black.

Look, even *this* body's changed!
Too certain of being different
from other men's clay
it moves contrarily,
silt in a wave:

At ten, the boy sits in the shallows,
splashes,
and sparkles in the spray,
is charmed
by mud on his toes
and her liquid gaze
lapping black beneath the clean
curve of his chin.

At twenty, the hero sports a beard and,
thinking to avoid reflections,
wanders the shore.
He seeks shelter
in a dark growth,
far from the camps
of other men.

At thirty, a father stumbles to the lake
and stares stubbornly down
at a tangle so knotted it hides
the hole in his chest.
There, mud-caked monsters
beat the skins of familial drums
and shadows sing to mermaids
and black-speckled loons.

At forty, he's empty and,
like other men,
looks for some other place
to fish.
He peers over the gunwales,
scratches his chin,
and the man glaring brokenly back
strokes a spot where
some charcoaled memory of youth
hangs graying in the mist.

It's not enough, he thinks,
to keep scissoring my way across this lake.
A boy could squander a lifetime
on these shores and gain
nothing
but a pocketful of sand
and some mussel shells.

Epiphany

Once
I saw layered
in each man's face
the scabs and scolding
sifted down through generations
like settling dust,
while as boys they slept,
comfortable and unsuspecting,
under sentiments common as clay,
but twice as hard to shake off.
I saw their dreams lilting
forgotten in
wrinkles that spread
like wild roots
or snow-ruin rutting
in spring boulders
still cold in the early sun.
I saw desire,
like a fossil,
compressed beneath the arching blue,
all the loess and alluvia
long ignored,
a geology of kin,
not stones.

Falling back here
I'm blind (shaking
dust from my hair)
and want a shovel.

Remembrance

That archeology student was so delicate:
the piggish grace in her small hands,
the well-shaped fingers white and smooth,
proportionate, typing cyphers on a laptop.
The keyboard beetles clicked.

Her fingertips were painted red.
Their exact warning did not look
lethal, much less Lazaric
to the dead—too soft, unedged—and yet
some shade shadows now this midden
of mid-aged memory.

that other time
another studied paths of stars,
believed prophetic speech,
despised our old entropic facts. She
killed his body, speaking otherworlds
to his no doubt imperfections.
I buried him with ointments, gold,
a boat fixed with a sail, then
conjured waves and dunes from time
and hid behind the pale.

Did she, her tapping, spill and
excavate that well-cursed tomb?
Do ghosts shallow so their sleep?
If she did not, is innocent
of such sirenic blame, am I
so free of sin that I can see
and not expect to haunt
the hallows of my history?

Honoring the Ancestors

My parents have spent twenty years
Looking backward under attic dust,
Weathering the churchyard's granite.
Meanwhile, certain where the good stuff lay,
I rushed headlong—
Only sideways glances—
Wondering why I stumbled,
Was always in debt.

I've seen them kneeling—
And boyish, pointed, giggled,
Looked away, shamelessly
Ashamed.
But I'm fifty-two this year, and I know
Where the village fool lives.

Seven decades drawn through their fingertips like pearls,
And this new luxury finds them sifting
The storied and forgotten. A god
Whose altar lay hidden in their future
Has set a deadfall down
In mine. It's inevitable
As carrion on the highway,
And I'm a crow.

They kneel with such grace,
Practiced and certain; I beat
The air with black wings,
Am raucous
With impatience, gluttony
(If I can find it). They bow
And sift and find
The nugget

They hold it out to me, glinting
Dimly in the faltered light. I see
The altar
Just down the road.

Eureka: Archimedes Remembers His Mother

In this morning's dim bath
he sees her
hiding,
her small displacements,
the mechanic lactations,
a dew that
waters deserts.

In the right season
this barren place
bursts yellow, reds explode,
lunar fuscias pop
amid small armaments—
threatening and protective—
bright defiances of the avid air.

But first the water:
cataclysm irrigates
sand, mud motionless
in dry arroyos
moves,
the greens green,
to something more akin.

She's been wet all his life:
waveless ocean
silent source
a lake murky
indistinct
present
passive.

Almost fifty
before her soft fulcruming
felt
for what it is:
a place to stand,
a lever long enough,
a world to move.

He Leaves This

I sip my hot, flavored coffee
on the cushioned seat
and deliberately avoid his eyes.
He shuffles pale sand and ash
between graying fingers, searching,
on this cold morning,
for some small length to burn
of unassailed comfort, a luxury
amongst the burnt and blotted ends.

Nothing within me could justify my looking,
no communion make connection
across this table,
the glass and brick,
the civilized path that beneath his feet
lies hard and unyielding.
He straightens to upright,
redistributes the weight of
his coat like Atlas,
and having found nothing here,
walks on.

That which I hoped to avoid is booming
its hollow presence within me,
a voided presence
left in the wake of passing.
Having found nothing
he leaves this, a gift,
and walks on.

Last Wish
> *I will die in Miami in the sun*
> —Donald Justice

He remembers,
tactile, untouchable as any history,
the bed sheets his mother hung
to dry in the lapping sun:
that bright cotton, patched.

Air flapping bleached them
stiff, soft and sandpapery,
summer warm
and so cool
on humming humid nights

he remembers dreaming,
smelling grass, cloud drift, that shroud
of day a momentary comfort
before he tumbled down the dark,
waiting as it did for him always.

He remembers
too late to save that sky, the hum
of summer trees, the way his mother
could fold into his boat the sun,
a sail across the dark.

Tonight, he wraps
his dreamless bundle by himself
and will a gravish wish.
For now, all he touches
is memory.

Dan Cullimore (1955-2017)—poet, advocate, craftsman, teacher—was a life-long resident of Columbia Missouri. Probably best known for his advocacy for neighborhoods, social justice, fair housing, and community gardens. Dan was a graduate of the University of Missouri. He spent many years working with young people struggling with mental health issues, with men's groups seeking wholeness, with community groups working to improve health and housing. He was an intelligent and articulate advocate for his friends and neighbors. Dan was also a skilled craftsman, whether his medium was wood or words. In both, he was largely self-taught. In wood, he built homes, drums, and tree houses. In words, he built poems.

www.ingramcontent.com/pod-product-compliance
Lightning Source LLC
LaVergne TN
LVHW041550070426
835507LV00011B/1026